U. S. DEPARTMENT OF AGRICULTURE
FARMERS' BULLETIN No. 1523

LEATHER SHOES
SELECTION AND CARE

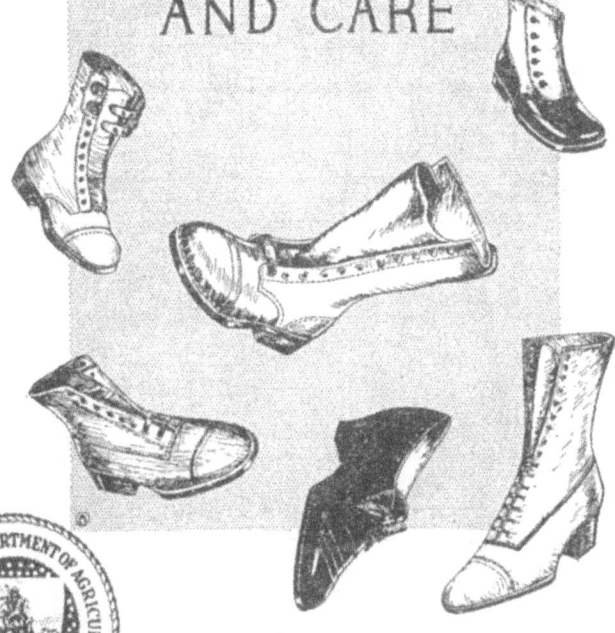

THIS BULLETIN contains information about the several kinds of shoe leather, gives suggestions for the judicious selection of leather shoes, and tells how to care for footwear in order to obtain the maximum service from it. It is a revision of and supersedes in part Farmers' Bulletin 1183.

Washington, D. C.   Issued April, 1927

LEATHER SHOES: SELECTION AND CARE

F. P. VEITCH, *Senior Chemist in Charge*, R. W. FREY, *Associate Chemist*, and H. P. HOLMAN, *Chemist, Leather and Tanning Investigations, Bureau of Chemistry*

CONTENTS

	Page		Page
Shoe leathers	1	How to care for shoes—Continued.	
Sole leather	1	Dyeing	18
Upper leather	2	Drying	18
Shoe construction	7	Oiling and greasing	19
How to select shoes	9	Waterproofing	19
How to care for shoes	16	Polishing	21
Repairing	16	Protection against mildew	21
Cleaning and renovating	17	Protection against alkaline substances	21

SHOE LEATHERS

SHOE LEATHERS are divided into two classes—bottom leather and upper leather. The bottom parts of a shoe, including the outsole, insole, welt, rand, and counter, are cut from bottom leather. The vamp, quarters, toe cap, and tongue, comprising the principal upper parts, are cut from upper leather.

As a rule, the uppers of a pair of shoes last much longer than the bottoms. The outsole and heel almost always wear out first, chiefly because they bear the brunt of the shoe's burden. Indeed, a pair of shoes made with welts, counters, and insoles of good-quality leather can usually be soled and heeled two or three times before the uppers give out. From the standpoint of wear and upkeep, therefore, the bottoms of a pair of shoes are more vital than the uppers.

SOLE LEATHER

Sole leather is made from heavy cattle hides. The best-wearing soles come from the bend, which is cut from a side or half hide of

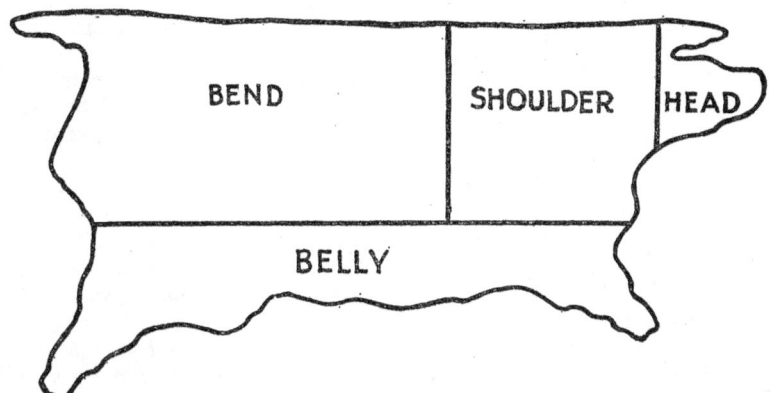

FIG. 1.—Sections of a side of leather

leather and is almost rectangular. The bend is about one-half of the side. It extends from the root of the animal's tail to just back of its shoulder and from the backbone to a nearly parallel line running through the top of the soft spots, or "breaks," at the fore and hind flanks. (Fig. 1.) Bends are about 50 inches long and 25 inches wide, although the exact size depends upon the size of the hide. Leather from the bend is close-fibered and firm. The poorest-wearing soles are cut from the belly (fig. 1), the leather from this section being flabby and soft. Experience and experiments have shown that the wear of a sole depends largely upon the section of the hide from which it was cut. Soles from the bend wear about twice as long as those from the belly and one and one-half times as long as those from the shoulder. When one or both soles on a pair of shoes wear out in an unreasonably short time it is often because they were cut from belly leather.

Most sole leather is vegetable tanned. Barks, woods, or nuts, and extracts of them are used for this tannage. The natural color of vegetable-tanned sole leather varies from tan to reddish brown. This leather is usually sold by the pound and is of a specified thickness, measured in "irons." An iron is a trade unit equivalent to one-forty-eighth of an inch. Outsole leather for Army shoes is at least 9 irons, or three-sixteenths of an inch, thick.

Some sole leather is made by tanning hides and skins with compounds of chromium. Chrome leather is not, as people often imagine, a leather substitute. In its natural state chrome sole leather has a light bluish-green color. When filled with waxes and greases the leather, now known as waxed chrome, is much darker. Chrome sole leather wears longer than vegetable-tanned sole leather, the natural or unwaxed being the longest-wearing sole leather made. Unwaxed chrome sole leather, however, is not suited for outdoor wear, except in very dry regions, because water quickly passes through it. Waxed chrome soles may be stiff at first, but the stiffness usually disappears after the shoes have been worn for a short time. Well-made waxed chrome soles are more than ordinarily durable, which makes them specially desirable for shoes for hard wear.

UPPER LEATHER

Trade names for shoe-upper leathers are bewildering. These names, however, refer more particularly to the grain, nature, and color of the finish of the leather than to the kind of skin from which it was made. The principal kinds of hides and skins used for upper leather are calf, goat, cattle, horse, and sheep. Kangaroo skins, pig skins, and shark skins are sometimes used.

Although very little chrome sole leather is now worn, about nine-tenths of all upper leather is chrome tanned.

Usually the finish is put on the grain or outer surface of the hide or skin, known also as the "hair side," although some upper leathers, like suède and waxed calf, are finished on the flesh side. Thick skins and hides are often split into two or more layers. The layer carrying the grain or hair side is a grain split and is made into grain leather. Grain leather, therefore, may or may not be a split. Even when it is a split it is seldom, if ever, referred to as such in

Fig. 2.—Natural grain of calf leather (magnified 5 times)

Fig. 3.—Natural grain of cowhide leather (magnified 5 times)

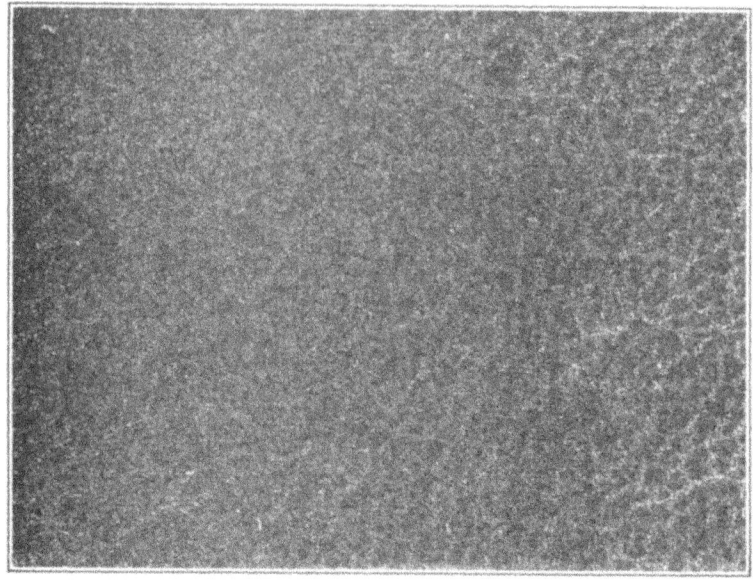

FIG. 4.—Natural grain of kidskin leather (magnified 5 times)

FIG. 5.—Natural grain of goatskin leather (magnified 5 times)

FIG. 6.—Natural grain of lambskin leather (magnified 5 times)

FIG. 7.—Natural grain of sheepskin leather (magnified 5 times)

the trade, the word "split" being reserved for the underlying layers. Grain leather makes better shoe uppers than do flesh splits.

Grain leather can often be recognized by its feel and general appearance, including the pattern or grain formed by fine lines or wrinkles and hair holes, scales, or other markings, depending upon the kind of skin from which the leather was made (figs. 2 to 7). Sometimes, however, the grain pattern of a certain skin is so cleverly embossed upon a skin of another kind that detection is very difficult.

The back of the human hand, particularly when examined under a slight magnification as with a reading glass, affords an excellent example of a skin pattern or grain.

Calfskin leather or calf leather is made from calfskins, these being defined as skins weighing not more than 15 pounds when green salted. Calf leather is pliable, of fine, smooth texture, and, as it is rarely split, very strong. All things considered, it probably makes the most satisfactory and serviceable upper leather for year-around wear. Much so-called calf leather of to-day is made from the heavier skins of older animals, ranging from veal and kipskins to the hides of full-grown cattle.

Side leather is made from cattle hides, generally cowhides, split to the desired thickness. The term "side" originated from the practice of cutting large hides into halves or sides before tanning. Although side leather does not have the natural elasticity, softness, and fine texture of calfskin leather, it makes a very durable upper and is extensively used, particularly for men's and boys' shoes.

Among the smooth-grain finishes for calf leather are dull gunmetal black and a bright or shiny glaze. Leather with a distinct, raised grain obtained by boarding, an operation that slightly puckers the surface, is known as boarded or box calf when finished black and as willow calf when finished in colors. Calf leather with a dull, wax finish on the flesh side is known as wax or dull calf; that with a dull but not waxy finish on the grain side, as mat calf.

Calf leather and side leather finished on the flesh side with a soft, velvety nap are called suède and ooze leather. Buffed leather is finished on the grain side with an emery wheel, which takes off part of the grain surface, leaving a softer finish. It has, however, a much less pronounced nap than suède.

Kid leather is rated among the excellent upper leathers. It is made from the skins of full-grown goats; not, as the name implies, from kidskins. Goatskins are seldom split, except possibly the butts of thick ones. Kid leather has a very fine, clear grain and is closely knit. It is softer and more pliable than calf leather and usually not so thick, for which reason it is not so warm and waterproof. Widely used for high-grade shoes, it is especially good for women's footwear. People with sensitive, tender feet generally find kid uppers more comfortable than calf, particularly in warm weather. Glazed kid is one of the most popular of shoe-upper leathers. Kid leather is also finished dull, as mat kid. Because of its many desirable features kid leather is often imitated in sheepskin, for which reason cheap kid shoes should be examined carefully before they are bought.

Sheepskin leather does not make a satisfactory upper leather, because, although very soft, it is loose and stretchy and not durable.

Shoe uppers of sheepskin leather soon get out of shape and scuff or peel, particularly at the toes. Sheepskin leather is used sometimes for the tops of cheap high shoes. It is used extensively for lining shoes, for which purpose it is very good.

Cordovan leather, made from the rump of the horsehide, is extremely close in texture, stiff fibered, and smooth and lacks the appearance of a grain characteristic of most other leathers. The finishing process gives it a reddish-brown color. It is probably the most durable of all upper leathers, and, because it is expensive, is frequently imitated. Sometimes leather is sold as cordovan when its only resemblance is the characteristic cordovan color. As this leather is fairly heavy, stiff, harsh, and nonporous it can not be worn by everybody. Its harshness sometimes causes ripping or cutting of the upper stitches.

Colt skins and horsehides, finished either dull or glazed, make very durable uppers and are particularly good for men's shoes.

Kangaroo skins make a very soft and fine, but expensive, leather somewhat like that from the best quality calfskins.

Patent leather is made by coating leather with special varnishes or enamels. Most patent leather is made from cattle hides, or side leather. Patent colt, from horsehides and colt skins, is of a superior quality. The varnished surface of patent leather gives a finish that for brightness, smoothness, and permanency of gloss can not be equalled by any other finish. Few manufacturers guarantee that the varnish film will not crack or peel, but patent leather is much better in this respect than it formerly was because of improvements in the processes of making and applying the finish. The film, however, deteriorates with age, losing its flexibility and developing fine checks. The leather is thoroughly stretched before varnishing, so that it has practically no give, and the finish is nearly air-tight and water-tight. Consequently patent leather sometimes proves uncomfortable.

SHOE CONSTRUCTION

The principal types of sewed shoes are known as " welted," " McKay," and " turned," according to the method of attaching the soles to the uppers. Those that are put together by wood or metal fasteners are called " pegged," " nailed," or " standard-screw " shoes.

The upper of the welted shoe is not attached directly to the sole, but both upper and sole are attached to a narrow strip of leather called a welt, which is first sewed to the upper and insole along its inner edge and later sewed to the outsole along its outer edge. Thus the welt, which should always be of exceptionally good leather, is the " keystone " that holds the shoe together. The exposed outer half of the welt which rests on the projecting part of the outsole should be smooth and should extend at least a quarter of an inch beyond the line where it joins the upper. Narrow welts and those finished by wheeling (fig. 8) often break and make repairing difficult and expensive. As a rule, welted shoes give longer service than other types, not only because on the average they are heavier but also because they can be more easily and more neatly repaired. Owing to the absence of tacks and stitches through the insole the inside finish of welted shoes is smooth.

The McKay shoe is made to a great extent in the lighter-weight and medium-price and cheaper grades. It has no welt. The outsole, upper, and insole are sewed together by stitches that pass through the insole. Consequently a row of stitches and also, because they can not be removed in the McKay construction, a line of clinched lasting tacks are left on the inside of the shoe. These at times hurt the feet. McKay shoes can not be as readily and as neatly repaired as welted shoes.

Turned shoes and slippers are very lightweight and flexible and are made chiefly for women and children. They have neither welt nor insole. The upper is sewed wrong side out to the sole and then turned right side out; hence the name "turned" shoe. In order to be able to turn the shoe after it is made, a very lightweight and flexible sole must be used. Turned shoes are not resoled and are not of the serviceable, durable type intended for hard wear.

About 40 per cent of all the leather and fabric footwear made in the United States is of the welt type, about 35 per cent is McKay,

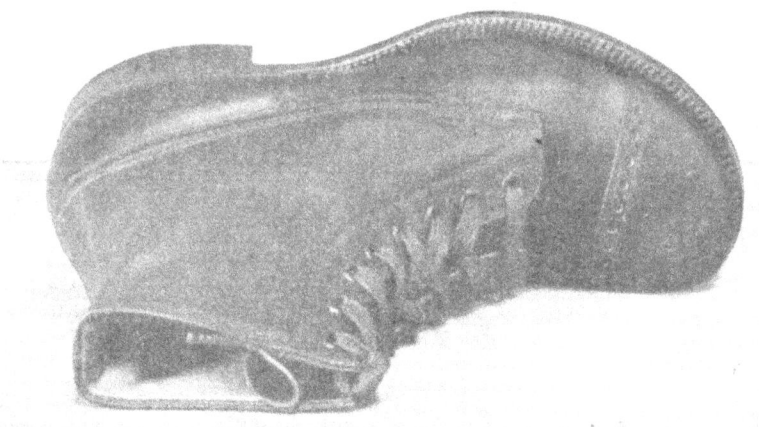

FIG. 8.—Shoe with wheeled welt

and 15 per cent is turned. The rest is divided between wood and metal fastened and "stitchdown" footwear. More than one-half of all slippers are of the McKay type and nearly all of the rest are turned. More than four-fifths of infants' shoes and slippers have turned soles.

Leather heels are built up in layers called lifts. Although the top lift, or the layer that comes in contact with the ground, is of good quality, firm leather, the other lifts are often of poor-quality leather, compressed leather scraps, or leather substitutes. The height of heels is expressed in eighths of an inch, an 8/8 heel being an inch high and an 18/8 heel, $2\frac{1}{4}$ inches high. The "breast" is the front face of the heel or the side toward the toes. The "pitch" of the heel is its angle or direction.

Rubber heels are now extensively worn. Substituted in part or entirely for the leather lifts, the rubber, in one piece, is nailed and cemented on the shoe. Rubber heels lessen the jar of walking, which makes them particularly popular in cities. Although as a rule they wear longer than leather heels, they slip more readily on smooth, wet surfaces, such as pavements, iron trapdoors, and car rails.

Wooden heels are covered with leather or fabric and are provided with a leather or rubber top lift. As a rule, wooden heels are not put on shoes of the most serviceable and durable types. Their use is confined almost entirely to lightweight footwear, because wood is not as heavy as leather or rubber.

Many styles of heels are used, particularly for women's shoes. Among the highest heels made are the French heel and the spike heel. The French heel has a deeply curved-in back edge, which spreads out to a small circular supporting area. The spike heel is suggestive of a spike, having a slender, straight-tapering body, coming to a very small base without any flaring. The Cuban heel may be as high as the French heel, although often it is not. It is unlike the French heel in that the back edge is not curved but tapers gradually; it differs from the spike heel in that the body is larger. The military heel is lower than the Cuban heel and also has a larger supporting area, because its back edge does not taper. The spring heel is very low. It is made by placing a wedge of leather between the heel seat of the shoe and the outsole. Many children's shoes have spring heels.

HOW TO SELECT SHOES

Most shoes are made over lasts built according to a schedule of standard measurements for the ball, waist, instep, and heel, the schedule being based upon the average proportions for normal feet (fig. 9). Shoes in which one or more of the foregoing parts are made larger or smaller, so that they do not correspond to the proportions of the standard schedule, are known as "combination-last" shoes. They are designed for better and more comfortable fitting of feet not of the usual proportions throughout.

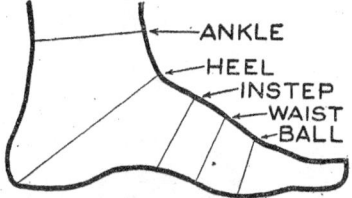

FIG. 9.—Where to measure the foot

The size of a shoe is its length for a standard width. The width is expressed in letters and the length in numbers. Stock widths range from triple A (AAA), the narrowest, to double E (EE), the widest. Whole sizes increase in length by one-third of an inch. The American size system runs from 0 to $13\frac{1}{2}$ in the first series and continues from 1 on in the second series. In the first series, size 0 is 4 inches long and size $13\frac{1}{2}$ is $8\frac{1}{2}$ inches long. In the second series, size 1 is $8\frac{2}{3}$ inches long and size 12 is $12\frac{1}{3}$ inches long.

Because of the desire of many people to wear shoes not over a certain size, regardless of the size of their feet, some shoe manufacturers have adopted code or secret numbering systems. In this way they are often able to render a real service in fitting the feet. Shape and fit are better guides to the right shoe than the size stamped on the lining. A certain size of one make or style of shoe may be a correct fit, whereas the same size of another make or style may not be.

The service to be required of shoes is an important factor in selecting footwear. The lightweight, fancy shoe or slipper has its place, but it obviously is not on the farm or the street, or in the office or shop.

Unfortunately, the purchaser of shoes can seldom correctly judge their quality and workmanship and the kind of leather from which they are made. Cheap shoes are not always an economy, nor are high-priced ones necessarily the wisest investment. Frequently a good share of the high cost goes simply for fancy workmanship and for novelty. About all the buyer can do is to rely on the reputation of the maker or dealer. Any reputable maker will stand back of the goods stamped with his name. Continued satisfaction with shoes can often be had by sticking to the make that has been found correct in design, comfortable in fit, and serviceable, and refusing to buy another pair put out by a manufacturer whose wares have been tried and found unsatisfactory.

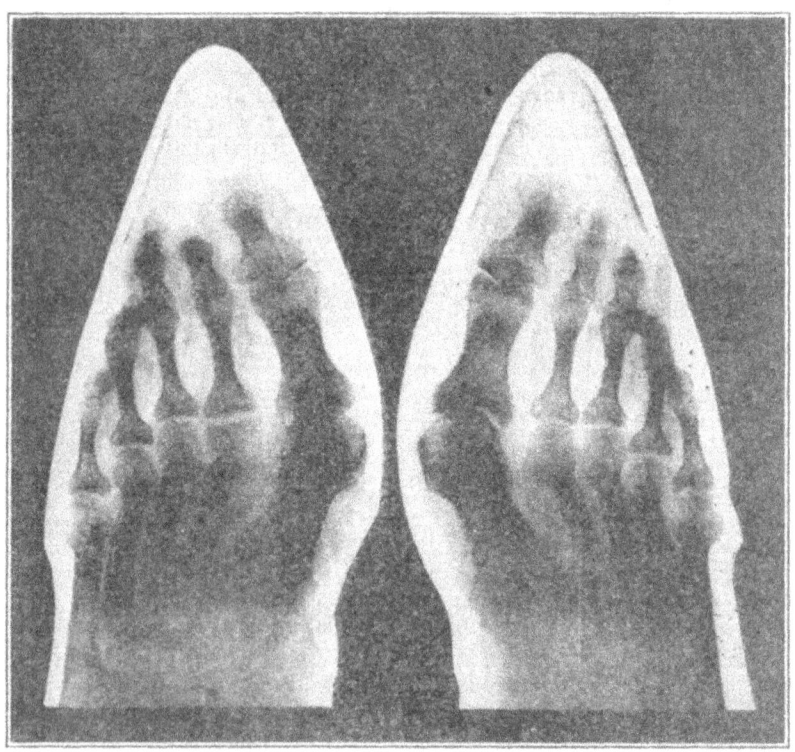

FIG. 10.—Effect of improperly shaped and ill-fitting shoes on the bones of the foot. (Photograph from Army Medical Museum.)

Although the fitting of shoes requires experience, judgment, and attention to details, many of the foot ills of to-day are caused by lack of thought on the buyer's part. We can not get around the fact that five toes need a certain space of a certain general shape if they are to spread out naturally and comfortably. When jammed into shoes with pointed, needlelike toes, the feet are sure to be cramped, twisted, and finally deformed. Toes are buckled and piled one on another and bones are bent. (Figs. 10 and 11.)

A baby does not need shoes until walking time. Shoes put on before then, generally for appearance, often do more harm than good. The first walking shoes should have flexible but firm soles, unpolished, preferably slightly buffed, and broad enough to be a steady platform under each foot. Very soft soles curl and make more difficult the baby's task of learning balance. Stiff or boardlike soles also are to be avoided. The toes of the uppers should be full or puffy and not, as they often are, so flat that the leather pulls straight back from the end of the sole and cramps the baby's toes.

The responsibility for the fitting of children's shoes falls upon parents, shoe dealers, and manufacturers. Very young children, of course, can not judge correctly the design and fit of their shoes. Older children are often willing to sacrifice comfort and money for what

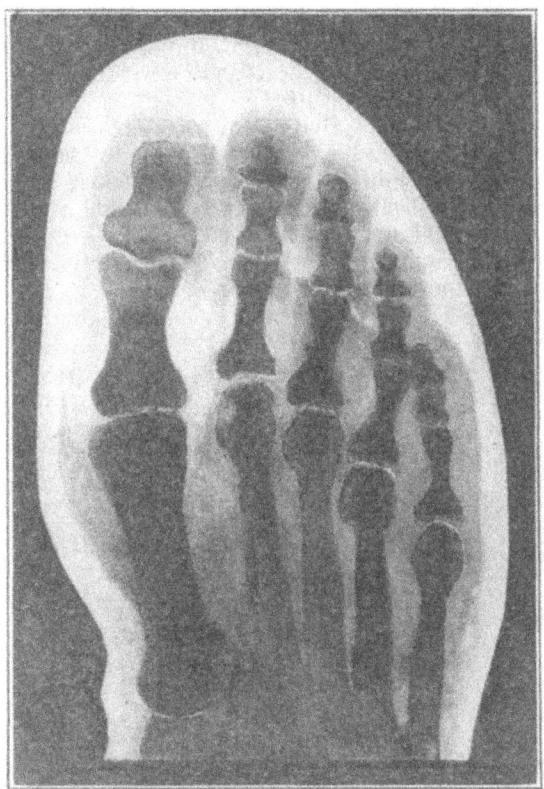

FIG. 11.—Effect of correctly shaped and properly fitting shoes on the bones of the foot. (Photograph from Army Medical Museum)

they consider a fashionable appearance. The young foot and its bones are easily twisted and bent out of shape by shoes that do not fit. Fortunately, during recent years, many manufacturers have been making children's shoes of correct design.

To be comfortable, safe, durable and attractive, shoes for everyday wear must conform to the natural shape of the feet and protect them. They must also provide a firm foundation for the body. The well-known Army shoe meets these requirements. Proceeding on the theory that an army is " only as good as its feet," the War

Department, after a lengthy study, worked out the type of shoe worn by the United States soldiers and Army nurses. (Fig. 12.) Civilian shoes made along the same lines, but of lighter-weight material and more pleasing appearance, can now be obtained in most parts of the United States. (Fig. 13.) They are well adapted for everyday wear in city and country alike. An increasing, persistent demand for such shoes is all that is needed to create an adequate supply of them.

Shoes of correct shape are broad and round at the toe and straight along the inner edge. (Fig. 14.) A pair of normal feet placed together touch at the heels and also from just in back of the big joints of the big toes up to the ends of these toes. The inner edges of the soles of a pair of properly made shoes do likewise. The more these edges diverge or curve toward the outside of the shoe (fig. 14), the more unnatural the shoe's shape and the greater the wearer's discomfort. If such shoes are persistently worn enlarged joints and bunions are almost sure to result.

Everyday shoes need soles that are at least moderately thick. Often the soles, particularly those of women's shoes, are so thin that walking with them on any but the smoothest of surfaces is painful. The feet soon become bruised and calloused. Thicker soles afford more protection to the feet not only against injury from sharp and uneven surfaces, but against water and slush as well. Furthermore, thicker soles last longer.

FIG. 12.—The U. S. Army shoe

A serviceable type, insuring maximum comfort and efficiency for the wearer, and well adapted for use in city and country alike. After a thorough study the War Department adopted this style of shoe for the U. S. Army.

Heels that are nearly as broad throughout as at the heel seat of the shoe, in other words, taper but little, are best for everyday shoes. Although the height may vary a little with the individual, high heels are frowned upon by most medical authorities. The heel of the Army nurse's shoe is $1\frac{1}{8}$ inches high. A sudden change from a high heel to a low one may cause discomfort at first. Such a change should be made gradually to give the feet and body time for adjustment. Failure to realize this has caused many a woman who has constantly worn high heels to think that she can not possibly wear low ones. The pitch of the heel is also important. Heels that slant too far forward can not steadily support the body or hold it in its proper posture.

Heels that are too narrow or too high or incorrectly pitched frequently cause weakened ankles, a wobbly walk, strained muscles, and slipping, twisting, and falling, with serious sprains and in-

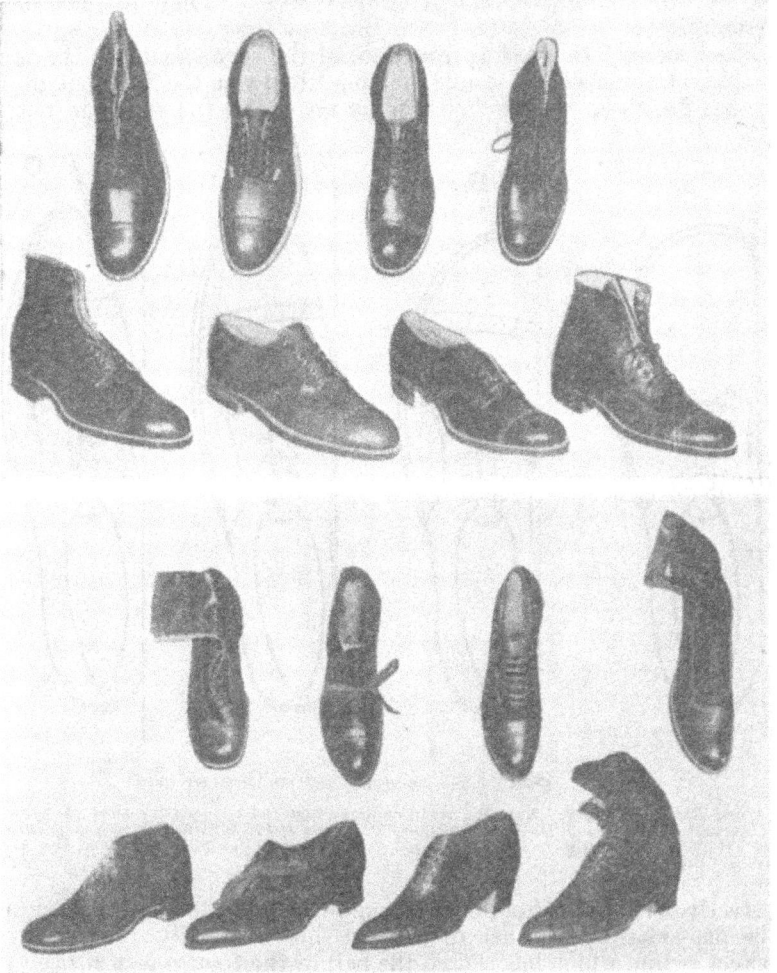

FIG. 13.—Attractive shoes of good shape

They combine comparatively straight inner lines, rounded toes, heels of medium height, and moderately thick soles, all of which make for greater serviceability, comfort, and safety.

juries at times. The weight is thrown upon the toes, and the feet are jammed into the fore part of the shoe, causing bruises, corns, weakened and crushed arches, and bent toes. The evils of high and narrow heels for women and girls, particularly those who are on their feet most of the day, can not be overemphasized. Such heels also soon run down on one side and frequently gap or pull loose from the shoe. Shoes with high narrow heels are more readily twisted out of shape than those with low broad heels, and are subjected to excessive strain on the seams and to uneven wear on both the soles and uppers.

Shoes should always be fitted with the entire weight of the body on the feet, as the feet are then at their largest. New shoes, if a correct fit, are comfortable from the start. They do not need "breaking in."

The "swing," or general direction, of the shoe should be the same as that of the foot; it should not tend to twist the foot out of its normal position. If the "swing" is not right, the shoe can not fit

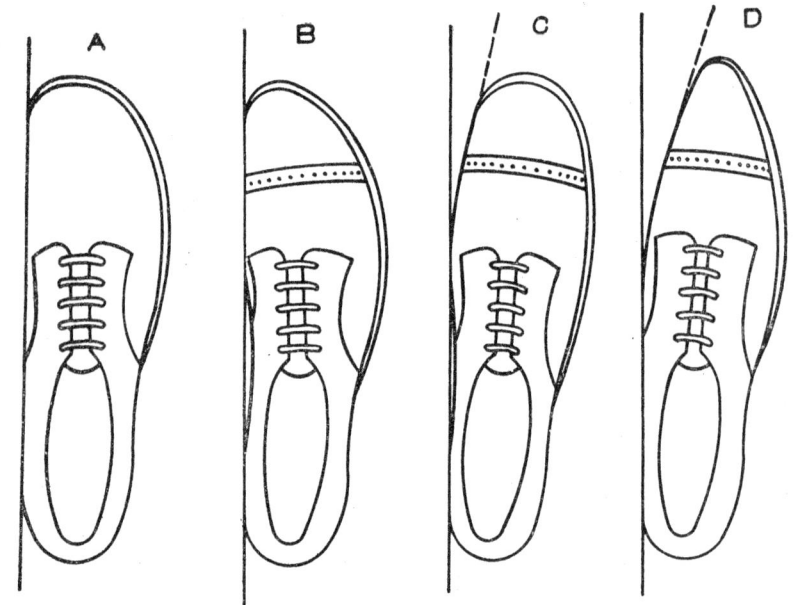

FIG. 14.—Shoes made on proper and on improper lines

A and B—Satisfactory. Note the straight inner line and rounded toe characteristic of the normal foot. C and D—Objectionable. Note the curve outward from the naturally straight inner line of the foot; also the too pointed toe D. (Photograph from the Army Medical Museum)

correctly. It will be too loose in one place and too tight in another. The one-sided appearance of a worn shoe is usually due to an incorrect swing, which has caused the ball of the foot to rest at one side of the shoe, rather than straight in the middle.

Shoes that fit correctly permit standing, walking, and quick turning in comfort and safety. A normal erect position of the body can be kept in such shoes without undue strain or discomfort. The feet, while snugly supported, are not cramped or crowded, and a firm, full tread is possible. Many shoes are too small for the wearer. This is an especially serious fault when they are too short. During wear a shoe may spread, but it will not become longer. There should be a good half-inch of empty space beyond the toes in a broad or well-rounded shoe. In more pointed shoes there should be more space.

Figure 15 shows the principal parts of a shoe. The broadest part should be at the end of the little toe. It is essential that the big joint of the big toe should come just at the rounding-in of the sole on the inside edge near the instep. This spot is one of the three important bearings of the foot, the corresponding part of the little toe and the heel being the other two. The vamp seam should not press upon the top of the foot back of the toes. Here there should always be a little, although not much, free space. The counter, which holds the back part of the shoe upper in shape, should center the heel of the foot in the heel seat of the shoe. It should fit the foot snugly and yet be wide enough to be comfortable when the whole weight of the body is borne by the feet for some time. Quarters should not

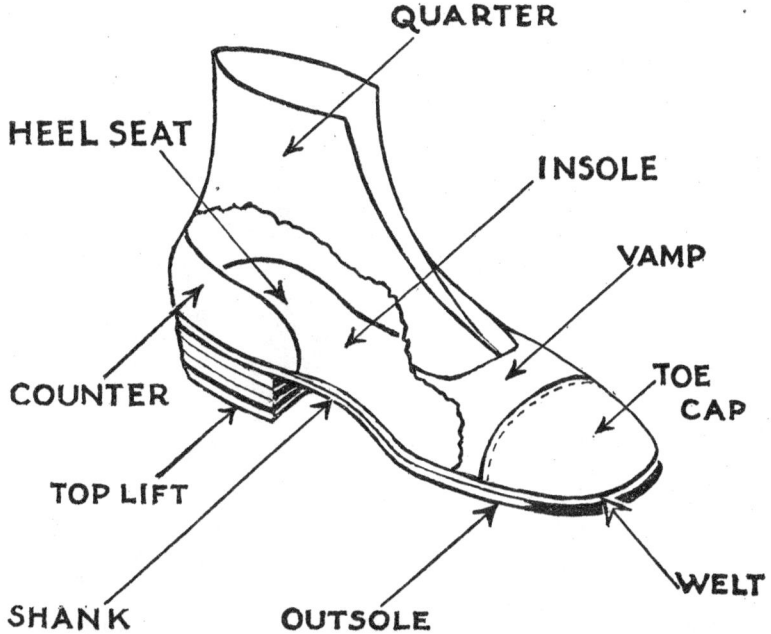

FIG. 15.—Principal parts of a shoe

be so full that the edges meet when the shoe is laced. There should be some space between those edges, so that the quarters may serve the purpose of holding the foot in place against the back of the shoe. However, the edges of the quarters should not gap so much that the pressure of the laces or buttons on the top of the instep will cause soreness.

Shoes that are too large are a misfit. With too much play in the shoe the foot is not snugly supported. Blisters are often formed, especially on the heel, by the rubbing of the foot against the inside of a shoe that is too large. Incidentally, neglect of foot blisters may result in serious infection.

Aside from any consideration of health and comfort, shoes for young and old alike are easier on the family budget if of correct design and fit. Such shoes do not soon lose their original attractiveness and shape and they wear longer.

HOW TO CARE FOR SHOES

The proper care of footwear, coupled with its intelligent selection, means a reduction of from one-quarter to one-half in shoe bills and at the same time keeps the feet neatly and serviceably shod. It is not necessary to discard shoes as soon as they begin to show signs of wear. After a seam has ripped or the outsole has worn through, shoes can often be repaired and worn for a long time.

Shoe trees help to keep shoes in their original shape. If they can not be had, the use of paper pads or stuffing is fairly satisfactory.

An economical plan is to have two pairs of shoes for alternate daily wear, thus permitting each pair to dry out between times. Perspiration is very hard on leather. Uppers constantly wet with

FIG. 16.—Repairing always should be done in time, certainly before the welt and insole become worn. Ordinarily it does not pay to repair shoes like these

perspiration may soon crack and rip, especially if not protected by occasional oiling.

Mud, water, or excessive dryness ruins leather; oil and grease preserve it. Therefore, the life of boots and shoes may be extended by keeping them clean, pliable, and water resistant. Those for farm or other heavy outdoor use need greasing. Those for street wear need polishing only, although the soles may be oiled or greased. Frequent polishing, especially with flexible wax polishes, keeps the leather soft and pliable and gives it a finish that helps to turn water and prevent the collection of dust and dirt. A light, even oiling with a little castor oil on a cheesecloth pad once or twice a month helps to keep patent leather uppers from cracking. Shoes thus cared for wear much longer than those that are neglected.

REPAIRING

Good care of shoes includes prompt repair. It is never true economy to wear down-at-the-heel, dilapidated shoes. Such shoes neither protect the feet nor properly support the body. What might be saved in leather may be paid eventually to foot specialists and doctors. The minute a seam begins to rip, the upper cracks through, a heel twists out of shape or runs down, or a hole wears through the outsole, the shoe needs mending. If the necessary bit of repairing is put off the shoe may be so badly worn that it is no longer worth mending and from $2 to $5 will be lost by neglect. (Figs. 16 and 17.) This is particularly true if the welt is worn away or the insole is worn through.

Heels should always be kept "squared up." When they begin to run down on one side both the shoes and the body are put under a strain. The shoes are soon permanently twisted out of their normal position and shape, and the feet, ankles, and legs may be twisted also. Unless the leather or rubber lift on wooden heels is promptly replaced when it wears away the covering of the wooden part is cut

FIG. 17.—Nevertheless, for $2 these shoes were put into excellent shape and were worn for another three months

through and may have to be replaced, sometimes an expensive job because of the difficulty of matching the material in the rest of the shoe.

Ripped seams in the uppers can frequently be stitched at home. A handy person, with the aid of a repair kit, can put on new heel lifts, rubber heels, half soles, and metal heel or toe plates without much difficulty. The equipment necessary for repairing shoes includes a last holder, three or four iron lasts of different sizes, a shoemaker's hammer, a pair of pincers, one or two leather knives, a leather rasp or file, awls, nails for soles and heels, flax shoe thread, bristles, and wax. These articles or made-up repair kits are sold by dealers in hardware or shoe findings and by some mail-order houses.

CLEANING AND RENOVATING

Butter, lard, vaseline, linseed oil, salad oil, and lubricating oil produce ugly stains on light-colored leather. Some attempts to remove such stains with gasoline or other ordinary grease solvents result only in spreading them. These spots can often be successfully removed by coating them with a thick solution of rubber in a solvent that evaporates quickly and then peeling off the rubber coating when it is almost dry, repeating the operation several times if necessary. A solution of finely chopped or shredded unvulcanized rubber (Para or Ceylon) in carbon bisulphide, in the proportion of 1 ounce of rubber to 8 fluid ounces of bisulphide, as well as some of the ready-prepared rubber cements, has been found satisfactory for this purpose. The cement must be very thick and dry very fast, and it must contain nothing but rubber and pure solvent. To keep the rubber from sticking too tight, the leather immediately around the stain may be moistened slightly with water just before applying the rubber solution. Carbon bisulphide should be used only where the ventilation is good and never near a flame. Its fumes are poisonous and inflammable.

All oil or grease spots should be removed as quickly as possible, particularly those made by linseed and other paint oils. These oils oxidize as they dry, so that they are soon only slightly soluble in the ordinary liquid solvents.

Milk spots leather and often leaves a white stain—sometimes a brown stain. Soap and water will remove the white stain, but no way of taking out the brown stain is known. The only feasible thing to do is to dye the leather a shade darker than the stain.

Now and then spots can be removed mechanically by the very delicate manipulation of a sharp edge, such as a safety-razor blade, or with fine emery or crocus cloth. As a rule this produces at least a slightly noticeable blemish. It may not be as unsightly as the stain, however.

Shoe polish sometimes accumulates on uppers. The appearance of such shoes can often be decidedly improved by cleaning with benzene or gasoline and repolishing.

Uppers with a suèdelike finish may become smooth and slick in spots. Often the nap can be satisfactorily raised with a small wire brush made for the purpose.

DYEING

Sometimes shoes may be dyed at home with one of the numerous ready-prepared dyes for leather now on the market. Many repair shops also dye shoes.

Some dye preparations contain nitrobenzene, which is recognizable by its penetrating almondlike odor. Such preparations may be entirely satisfactory for dyeing, but, as nitrobenzene is poisonous, they never should be applied to shoes while on the feet. Absorption of nitrobenzene through the feet may cause illness and even death.

In applying dye preparations at home it is sometimes helpful to experiment with them on cast-off shoes. This gives an idea of the effect and of the best method of application.

DRYING

Shoes are easily damaged when wet. Wet leather is soft, so that it readily stretches out of shape and stitches cut through it easily. It wears away rapidly.

Wet shoes must be dried very carefully, for wet leather "burns" much more readily than dry leather. If the leather becomes hotter than the hand can bear it is almost sure to be ruined. People often unwittingly spoil their shoes by placing them while wet against hot radiators in street cars, against hot steam pipes or stoves, or even in hot ovens. When dried too fast and without care, shoes shrink and become hard, tight, and out of shape. The sole often cracks and sometimes even falls out in pieces.

The right way to dry shoes is as follows:

First wash off all mud and grit with tepid water. Oil or grease work or rough shoes with one of the preparations described on page 20 or with something similar. Oil street shoes with castor oil. (If the castor oil on a piece of cheesecloth is applied lightly and evenly and well rubbed in, the shoes will take a good shine when dry. If too much oil is used, polishing will be difficult.) Then straighten the counter, heel, vamp, and toe, and stuff the shoes with crumpled paper to keep the shape and hasten drying. Finally set the shoes aside in a place that is not too warm and let them dry slowly.

Never put them close to a hot stove or radiator, and do not wear them until they are thoroughly dry. It is a good plan to polish street shoes once or twice as soon as they are dry.

OILING AND GREASING

The rational use of suitable oils or greases will make shoes wear much longer than they otherwise would. Shoes worn on farms, in forests, and in mines are helped by oil or grease whenever the leather begins to harden or dry or fails to turn water well. This treatment not only makes them last longer but, when the shoes are well made of good materials, keeps the feet dry as well.

Among the best materials for greasing shoes are neat's-foot, cod, and castor oils, tallow, and wool grease, or mixtures of them. Any one may be applied in the following way:

First brush the soles and uppers thoroughly to remove all dust and dirt and then warm the shoes carefully, bearing in mind the danger of burning them if they are wet. Apply the warm oil or grease, which should never be hotter than the hand can bear, with a swab of wool or flannel, and rub it well into the leather, preferably with the palm of the hand. Take special care to work the grease in thoroughly where the sole is fastened to the upper, as water soaks through there most often. Let the greased shoes dry in a warm, but not hot, place.

WATERPROOFING

Waterproofed footwear can not be expected to keep the feet perfectly dry if worn for a long time in wet weather, nor will it take the place of rubber overshoes or boots for walking in water, slushy snow, or very soft mud. Nevertheless, waterproofed, properly made leather shoes are satisfactory for protecting the feet during rain or snow storms and for use on wet pavements or wet ground where there are no deep puddles. They keep in the perspiration to a large extent, but are less objectionable than rubber footwear in this respect.

Grease for waterproofing shoes in summer should be harder than that used in winter. Because heavily greased shoes have a tendency to cause the feet to perspire and swell in hot weather and because there is less need for water-resistant shoes during such weather, it is rarely advisable to put on as much grease then as in winter and spring. In summer the quantity of grease used should not exceed the quantity that the leather will take up without leaving a greasy surface. In winter a mixture of grease and oil that is not too hard when cold is required, and more of it than the leather will absorb may be used, especially if the maximum water resistance is desired. An excess does no harm in winter.

WATERPROOFING FORMULAS

For waterproofing shoes, nothing better than the following simple formulas is known to the Department of Agriculture. The department believes that these formulas infringe on no existing patents or pending applications for patents, but it can assume no responsibility in the matter.

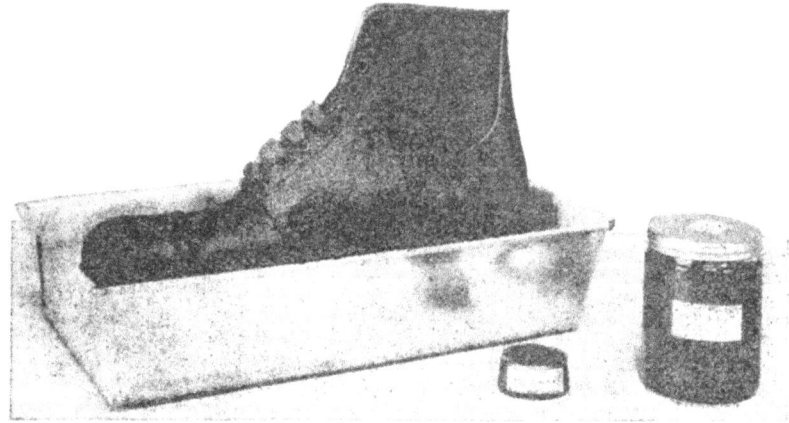

FIG. 18.—All you need for waterproofing shoes

Formula 1

Natural wool grease	ounces	8
Dark petrolatum	do	4
Paraffin wax	do	4

Formula 2

Petrolatum	pound	1
Beeswax	ounces	2

Formula 3

Petrolatum	ounces	8
Paraffin wax	do	4
Wool grease	do	4
Crude turpentine gum (gum thus)	ounces	2

Formula 4

Tallow	ounces	12
Cod oil	do	4

Melt together the ingredients by warming them carefully and stirring thoroughly. Apply the grease when it is warm, but never hotter than the hand can bear.

Grease thoroughly the edge of the sole and the welt, as this is where shoes leak most, and completely saturate the sole with the grease. This can be done most conveniently by letting the shoes stand for about 15 minutes in a shallow pan containing enough of the melted waterproofing material to cover the entire sole. (Fig. 18.) Rubber heels, however, should not be put in the grease, because it softens them. To waterproof the soles of shoes with rubber heels use a pie pan to hold the melted grease and set the shoes astraddle the rim of the pan with the heels outside.

POLISHING

Most shoe polishes are mixtures of waxes, colored with dyes and softened to a pasty consistency, usually with turpentine. Others that contain no turpentine are made by boiling mixtures of waxes with a solution of borax or soda, colored with a dye or finely pulverized bone charcoal, and adding either a solution of ordinary soap to form a paste or a solution of castile soap to form a liquid. Some liquid polishes consist of shellac, waxes, and dye in an alcoholic solution.

The statement sometimes made that shoe polishes containing turpentine are injurious to leather has not been borne out by experiments with several polishes of this kind. Now and then the turpentine becomes rancid, acquiring a sharp, disagreeable odor and making the polish gummy. Such polishes give less satisfactory shines than those in which the turpentine is sweet. Many liquid polishes contain nitrobenzene, which can be recognized by its almond-like odor. Such preparations may be entirely satisfactory as polishes; but as nitrobenzene is poisonous, they never should be applied to shoes while on the feet.

Polishes containing free acid or alkali may be harmful to leather. They sometimes cause cracking of the vamp where the shoe is bent most often. Liquid cleaners that contain oxalic acid, often put up in combination with paste polishes for use on light-colored shoes, usually injure the leather.

It is possible to detect free acid or alkali, in a polish that does not contain water-soluble dye, by stirring some of the polish with warm rain water and testing the clear water after settling with red and blue litmus paper. A change of the color of the paper from red to blue indicates free alkali; a change from blue to red indicates free acid. If the polish contains water-soluble dye, free acid and alkali can be detected only by chemical analysis.

Shoe uppers that have been oiled and greased with any oil other than castor oil can not be polished satisfactorily. If castor oil is applied lightly, the shoes may be polished after they have been left for from 12 to 24 hours to give the leather time to take up the oil. Sometimes only the soles are greased, care being taken to get no grease on the uppers. Thus the shoes are made fairly water resistant and at the same time they will take a shine well.

PROTECTION AGAINST MILDEW

Shoes kept in a warm, damp, and dark place are almost certain to mildew. Mildew probably will not seriously harm the shoes unless it is allowed to remain too long, but it may change their color. The simplest way to prevent mildewing is to keep the shoes in a well-ventilated, dry, light place. When first detected, the mildew should be washed off with soap and warm water, or simply wiped off with a moist cloth and the leather well dried. The application in the home of preparations designed to prevent mildew is not recommended.

PROTECTION AGAINST ALKALINE SUBSTANCES

Lime, Portland cement, lye, and other alkaline substances quickly ruin leather. Shoes worn by people working with such substances will last much longer if kept well greased.

ORGANIZATION OF THE
UNITED STATES DEPARTMENT OF AGRICULTURE

July 2, 1928

Secretary of Agriculture	W. M. JARDINE.
Assistant Secretary	R. W. DUNLAP.
Director of Scientific Work	A. F. WOODS.
Director of Regulatory Work	WALTER G. CAMPBELL.
Director of Extension	C. W. WARBURTON.
Director of Personnel and Business Administration	W. W. STOCKBERGER.
Director of Information	NELSON ANTRIM CRAWFORD.
Solicitor	R. W. WILLIAMS.
Weather Bureau	CHARLES F. MARVIN, *Chief*.
Bureau of Animal Industry	JOHN R. MOHLER, *Chief*.
Bureau of Dairy Industry	L. A. ROGERS, *Acting Chief*.
Bureau of Plant Industry	WILLIAM A. TAYLOR, *Chief*.
Forest Service	R. Y. STUART, *Chief*.
Bureau of Chemistry and Soils	H. G. KNIGHT, *Chief*.
Bureau of Entomology	C. L. MARLATT, *Chief*
Bureau of Biological Survey	PAUL G. REDINGTON, *Chief*.
Bureau of Public Roads	THOMAS H. MACDONALD, *Chief*.
Bureau of Agricultural Economics	LLOYD S. TENNY, *Chief*.
Bureau of Home Economics	LOUISE STANLEY, *Chief*.
Plant Quarantine and Control Administration	C. L. MARLATT, *Chief*.
Grain Futures Administration	J. W. T. DUVEL, *Chief*.
Food, Drug, and Insecticide Administration	WALTER G. CAMPBELL, *Director of Regulatory Work, in Charge*.
Office of Experiment Stations	E. W. ALLEN, *Chief*.
Office of Cooperative Extension Work	C. B. SMITH, *Chief*.
Library	CLARIBEL R. BARNETT, *Librarian*.

This bulletin is a contribution from

Bureau of Chemistry and Soils	H. G. KNIGHT, *Chief*.
Chemical and Technological Research	C. A. BROWNE, *Chief*.
Technochemical Division	F. P. VEITCH, *Senior Chemist, in Charge*.

ADDITIONAL COPIES
OF THIS PUBLICATION MAY BE PROCURED FROM
THE SUPERINTENDENT OF DOCUMENTS
U. S. GOVERNMENT PRINTING OFFICE
WASHINGTON, D. C.
AT
5 CENTS PER COPY

▽

www.ingramcontent.com/pod-product-compliance
Lightning Source LLC
Chambersburg PA
CBHW031440040426
42444CB00006B/907